FIRST READER,

FOR

YOUNG CHILDREN.

CONSISTING OF

PROGRESSIVE LESSONS

IN

READING AND SPELLING

MOSTLY IN

EASY WORDS OF ONE AND TWO SYLLABLES

BY WILLIAM H. McGUFFEY,
Professor in Miami University, Oxford

Editions 1836 - 1853

CINCINNATI:
PUBLISHED BY TRUMAN AND SMITH
150 MAIN STREET

ROMAN NUMERALS EXPLAINED

A numeral is a symbol meaning number. Our system of counting is believed to have begun by people counting on their fingers. Both the Arabic (1, 2, 3, 4, etc.) and the Roman (I, II, III, IV, etc.) are believed to have started this way. The word digit, meaning number, is from the Latin word digitus, meaning finger. The number V (5) seems to be representative of an open hand; the number X (10) seems to be like two open hands.

In earlier days, our forefathers used the Roman system to indicate chapter headings in books. To help you understand those numbers more easily you may refer to the chart below:

Roman	Arabic	Roman	Arabic	Roman	Arabic
I	1	XI	11	XXX	30
II	2	XII	12	XL	40
III	3	XIII	13	L	50
IV	4	XIV	14	LX	60
V	5	XV	15	LXX	70
VI	6	XVI	16	LXXX	80
VII	7	XVII	17	XC	90
VIII	8	XVIII	18	C	100
IX	9	XIX	19	D	500
X	10	XX	20	M	1000

Editors: Raymond S. Moore
Dorothy N. Moore
Jane Thayer

Illustrations by Greg Constantine

ISBN 0-913717-01-0
Printed in the United States of America

THE NEW MOORE-McGUFFEYS

That Wm. McGuffey's readers have done more than their share of building American character and literacy is generally conceded. Yet it is also widely held that some of their stories are out of step with the times, such as those which suggest that Indians are savages, or that a little boy was "gay" (i.e. joyful), or that God doesn't love little boys who are naughty. Many ecologically-minded citizens are also unhappy with the stories that describe whaling escapades; blood foaming on the billows, etc.

The Moore editions. These McGuffey Readers omit such stories from the original (1836) versions and substitute more acceptable accounts from the 1838, 1843 and 1853 editions. But the Moore editors went beyond these changes to offer better word lists, questions which require more thought, and—particularly in Reader IV—bright, updated introductory remarks to great pieces of literature. Added to these changes are original paintings in color for the first two books and a strong cloth binding, and you have a superior set of readers.

What the McGuffeys really do. Remember that the four standard Wm. McGuffey Readers cover grades one through twelve for most students. Most critics agree that the McGuffey primers and spellers are not of unusual value. In the last century children went to school only about three months each year, and then often only half a day. They did not start until at least age 8 and often 12 or 14. Usually the first McGuffey Reader was used the first year for content and again the second year for elocution (expression). Each reader was thus used for two years, unless the students were late starters, in which event they moved through them much faster.

HOW TO USE THE MOORE-McGUFFEYS

Your modern child will benefit from the use of these old-fashioned books if you will precede their use with teaching the letters and their sounds, informally at first. Provide simple phonics materials when your child begins to show an interest in learning about sounds. It is usually not necessary to buy $100 or $200 phonics programs. With a minimum of materials you can introduce your child to letter symbols and what they "say."

Arm yourself with a basic guidebook like *Five Homespun Steps to Teach Your Child To Read.* Use newspaper advertisements, cereal boxes or even roadsigns for your "lesson books." You might want to label household items like door, window, stove, etc., in a game-like method with your child. Concentrate on one or two letters for a short period of time, emphasizing the *sound* of the letter rather than the name. Helpful teaching aids include a mirror for your child to see the placement of his tongue, lips and mouth as he follows your example, large letter cards to place on the wall, a pan of cornmeal for "writing" the letters and small (1″) letter cards (lower case) for your child to manipulate into place as you slowly dictate a word, sound-by-sound.

ROLE OF SIGHT READING

While phonics instruction lays a firm foundation for reaching and provides the child with tools for unlocking most unknown words, phonics alone does not provide a complete reading base. Eventually your child must become so familiar with well known words that he/she can say them and gain meaning from them as easily and simply as recognizing the family cat.

Build your child's early enthusiasm for reading by having field trips, store excursions, or events with the family pet, turning them into stories, reports or booklets. You can function as scribe while your child dictates familiar happenings. If you need detailed instructions in how to do this, use the *Creative Writing Guide's* step-by-step instructions. See *Family Report* Order Form.

To utilize this teaching tool to the fullest, draw your child's attention to the words dictated in the story which follow phonics rules previously learned. Sometimes a more general question like, "Can you find a word with a 'permission e' in this sentence?," will give your little student more challenge. (A good example would be changing "cap" to "cape," with "e" making /a/ say a.)

From 2 months to a year after you have begun following these phonics instructions, your child should be able to begin reading the first *Moore-McGuffey Reader.*

Following these suggestions will help you to utilize the *Moore-McGuffeys* to their fullest potential:

1. Help your child pronounce each word in the word list at the *end* of the chapter.

2. Discuss the meaning of the words. (For variety you may ask the meaning of the word *after* it is read in context. This is an excellent method for learning definitions.)

3. Require spelling mastery of these words.

4. Allow your child time to read the story silently.

5. Ask questions about the story. Relate as many questions as possible to your child and how he/she would feel or react to similar circumstances. The "how" and "why" questions are particularly important.

6. Let your child tell the story next day in his/her own words. Observe speaking quality, posture and interest.

7. Ask your child to read the story aloud. Be especially watchful if your child manifests nervous habits. The following habits may be warning signs that reading is a stressful struggle, with "burn-out" a strong possibility.
    A. Curls corners of the book.
    B. Clears throat frequently.
    C. Fidgets in his chair.
    D. Twists lock of hair.
    E. Holds book too close or too far.
    F. Squints or frowns.
    G. Skips words or lines.

8. Use the following list of possible oral reading problems and short remedial suggestions as your child reads.

A. Poor word-by-word phrasing. Print "flasher lists" of phrases to be read. For example "in the," "over the," "a dog."
B. Monotone – demonstrate lots of inflection as *you* read.
C. Pitch – too high or too low. Use cassette recorder. Alternate short reading samples. Play back.
D. Volume – too loud or too soft. Use cassette recorder.
E. Loses place, skips. Hold card under the line being read. Use a pointer or small penlight moved slowly along the line.
F. Ignores punctuation. Color large red dots over periods and commas. Demonstrate pauses dramatically as *you* read the selection.

We trust these simple suggestions will help you experience the joy of reading discovery with your child. Don't forget to relax, and be happy as you learn together.

McGUFFEY'S FIRST READER: INTRODUCTION

Nearly 150 years ago, William Holmes McGuffey gathered his own writings, clippings from periodicals and selections from standard works, and wrote the first four McGuffey READERS. Drawing upon the areas of family life, farming, science, history, biography and secular and Biblical literature, he presented his readers with a wide range of interests—an even wider range than is found in today's typical reading books.

After the READERS were published in 1836, and until 1920, more than 120 million copies were sold; it is estimated that each copy was read by five to 10 students. Since 1920, McGuffey's READERS have continued to sell and be used by schools and parents concerned about the contents of children's textbooks.

The distinctive McGuffey contribution, remembered by yesterday's readers and sought by today's concerned parents and teachers, is found in his emphasis on moral values. More than half of McGuffey's lessons center around those values.

In a nation where the motto is "In God We Trust," McGuffey logically focused on God. He considered a child's personal relationship with God to hold great significance. His stories, therefore, extolled—and enticed the child to—a God-centered life.

To help a child find happiness, make decisions and set priorities, McGuffey's lessons stressed that a child's first considerations must be to do right and be good. He praised the virtues of self-denial and obedience. READER stories accent piety, honesty, kindness to people and animals, thrift, industry and patriotism.

McGuffey's READERS handle morals much differently from today's classroom textbooks, some of which present—without comment—all forms of lifestyles and behaviors. McGuffey did not back away from confronting his young students with moral dilemmas; the dilemmas, however, were always within the students' abilities and powers to resolve. He required responsible decisions and correct behavior of children, but only within their capabilities. McGuffey believed that when children become adults, they carry their already-practiced senses of moral responsibility into a larger arena.

Written and published before the days of ethnic awareness, the READERS are peopled only by Anglo-Saxon children. But the children represent all socio-economic levels.

Also, the women who appear in the stories are not portrayed in subservient positions. McGuffey realized adults enter the child's world as instructors or interpreters of the natural and social worlds rather than lawyers, doctors, housewives or professors.

EDITORIAL GUIDELINES

Selections for this "Best of McGuffey" edition were made by choosing the best stories in the original edition and in the 1853 edition which McGuffey approved. We edited punctuation, capitalization, spelling and usage to reflect present standards and corrected certain discrepancies and omissions.

When considering selections, carefully-set standards led us to omit or amend stories from each READER with:

1) Poor literary quality or duplicated subjects.

2) References to violence or cruelty to people or animals.

3) Highly didactic lessons and over-moralizing expositions.

4) Demeaning language to describe various ethnic, religious or socio-economic groups.

5) Controversial theological material.

6) Unrealistic or questionable credibility.

7) Passages suggesting children are loved only when they are good.

8) Common information that today's child would have already learned from other sources.

To give the child a sense of heritage, the viewpoint and vocabulary generally have been retained, although 20th century technology has made some discussion obsolete.

The questions at the end of each lesson have been completely rewritten. They speak to today's child from today's viewpoint, but still accomplish McGuffey's purpose—to increase reading comprehension and reasoning power, and to reinforce the lesson. The questions also help the child understand how technology has changed today's lifestyle from that of yesterday's.

Each lesson's word list has been checked to eliminate duplication and to insure that each word appears in the lesson studied. Lists may be used for at least three purposes: as new reading words, as spelling words or as new vocabulary words.

For the first time in their long history, McGuffey READERS are illustrated in color. The all-new illustrations created for this edition have been produced in keeping with the hues and combinations of McGuffey's times. For this edition, artist Greg Constantine captures the action of the stories and portrays them in settings true to their historical period.

Thus our editorial policy has been to present the 20th century child the same books that served as foundation stones in the development of the American character and the elevation of the nation's standards of literacy.

We present to today's child the READERS of the original editor—William Holmes McGuffey. (For a biographical sketch of McGuffey, see the appendix.)

Dennis R. Moore, Publisher

CONTENTS

LESSON I (1)

The New Book

Do you see that boy?

There are two girls with him.

The name of the boy is John.

The names of the girls are Ann and Jane.

Jane has a book in her hand.

They can all read from the book.

They must keep the book clean.

They must see how fast they can learn.

LESSON II (2)

This boy has a bird.
The bird is on his hand.
Some birds can talk.

The dog barks.
Do you hear the dog bark?
Boys and girls play with dogs.

The boys run fast.
They run as fast as they can.
One of the boys has no hat.

Here is a small dog.
He has the boy's hat.
The boys cannot get it.

LESSON III (3)

This horse eats hay.
The hay is on the ground.
Hay is made of grass.

The two girls go to school.
The bags are for their books.
Do you go to school?

This cow is in the pond.
The cow gives us milk.
You must not hurt the cow.

The hen eats corn.
The hen picks up the corn.
Can the little chicks eat corn?

LESSON IV (4)

The Wild Ox

An ox has two horns. He has four legs and four feet.

A wild ox will toss boys on his horns.

The ox pulls the plow and the cart. He is large and strong,

and he works hard for man.

An ox has red, white, or black hair. He eats grass, hay, corn, and drinks water.

He lies down on his side when he sleeps.

– – –

ox	has	two	horns
he	four	legs	feet
and	hard	man	hay

LESSON V (5)

The Boy and the Dog

This dog stands on his feet. He wants to play with John.

A dog has four feet. A dog and a cat can see in the dark.

The dog keeps watch at night and barks.

Dogs bark most when the moon shines.

A dog will chase a sheep or hog or cow and bite it.

If you are kind to the dog, he will not bite you.

– – –

feet	wants	bark	dog
cat	cow	sheep	kind

LESSON VI (6)

The Bear

Did you ever see a bear? A bear has long, brown hair and a short tail.

The bear has large paws. He lives in a den in the woods.

The bear can run up a tree, like Puss. He is very strong and may be cross. We call the bear, Bruin.

LESSON VII (7)

Time To Get Up

Mamma, may I get up?

Yes, my child, you may. The sun is up and the dew has gone off the grass. It is cool now, but it will soon be hot. When the sun gets up high, it will be warm.

I will go out on the porch and spin my top.

– – –

yes	when	now	up
out	warm	sun	porch
child	grass	hot	cool

LESSON VIII (8)

Little Henry

Well, Henry, what have you read in your new book?

I read of three boys who went to school.

Each of them had a fine, large cake. James ate so much that it made him sick. George kept his so long that it got dry and was not fit to eat.

But John gave some of his cake to each of his schoolmates and then took a piece himself. He gave the rest to an old, blind man.

The old man could not see to work for his food. So John gave him a share of his cake.

How kind John was! I love kind boys and girls.

– – –

book	poor	John	share
dry	blind	made	have
long	cake	then	that
large	sick	kept	much
Henry	James	George	boys

LESSON IX (9)

The Poor Old Man

Jane, there is a poor old man at the door.

He asks for something to eat. We will give him some bread and cheese.

He is cold. Will you give him some clothes, too?

I will give him a suit of old clothes, which will be new to him.

Poor man! I wish he had a warm house to live in and kind friends to live with him; then he would not have to beg from door to door.

We should be kind to the poor. We may be as poor as this old man and need as much as he.

Shall I give him some money to buy a pair of shoes?

No, you may give him a pair of shoes.

It is hard for the poor to have to beg from house to house.

Poor boys and girls sometimes have to sleep out-of-doors all night. When it snows they are very cold, and when it rains they get quite wet.

– – –

Who is it that gives us food to eat and clothes to make us warm?

It is God, my child. He makes the sun to shine and

sends the rain upon the earth that we may have food.

God makes the little lambs bring forth wool, that we may have clothes to keep us warm.

– – –

God	poor	some	eat
old	asks	man	give
money	him	bread	cheese
cold	will	should	you
shine	hard	pair	shoes
sleep	Jane	little	lamb

LESSON X (10)

The Sun Is Up

See, the sun is up. The sun gives us light. It makes the trees and the grass grow.

The sun rises in the east and sets in the west. When the sun rises, it is day. When the sun sets, it is night.

This little boy was up at five. He saw the sun rise and heard the sweet songs of birds on every bush.

Do you know who made the sun?

God made it.

God made the moon and all the stars. How good God is to us. He gives us all we have and keeps us alive.

We should love God.

God sees and knows all things because God is everywhere. He sees me when I rise from my bed and when I go out to walk and play. When I lie down to sleep at night, He keeps me from harm.

Though I do not see the wind, yet it blows around me on all sides. God is with me at all times, and yet I see Him not.

– – –

sun	grass	bird	then
east	west	five	rise
see	play	keeps	heard

LESSON XI (11)

The Cat and the Dog

Do you see the cat and the dog? We call a cat, Puss.

Puss has run up on the wall. The dog barks, but he cannot catch her.

Puss has sharp claws and sharp teeth.

If you pull her hair or tail, she will scratch or bite you.

Give Puss some milk; then she will love you. Little boys and girls should not hurt the dog or the cat.

– – –

cat	milk	pull	hair
dog	love	teeth	give
Puss	you	barks	little

LESSON XII (12)

The Walk

Come Mary, get your bonnet and we will take a walk.

See, the sun is in the west. It is going to set. How large it looks. We may look at it now. It is not as bright now as when it was up high in the sky. It will soon lie out of sight. Now it is quite gone.

How red the clouds are. We can see the moon and all the pretty stars when the sun sets. The moon is not as bright as the sun.

See the bright stars. Some of the stars are as large as the world, but they are so far away that they look small.

Papa, is the sun as large as the world? Yes, my child, and a great deal larger, but it is a great way off.

– – –

bonnet	high	away	Mary
walk	sky	small	pretty
take	now	make	look
come	gone	red	large

LESSON XIII (13)

Robert and His Horse

Here is a fine horse.

Has the horse been fed?

Give him some hay and some oats.

The horse lives on grain; he does not eat meat. Bears eat

meat and dogs eat meat, but horses and sheep and cows do not.

May I ride on the horse? No, you are too small. When you grow to be as big as Robert you may ride.

– – –

horse	fine	hay	oats
grain	meat	ride	grow
small	when	you	eat

LESSON XIV (14)

The Wild Beasts

James and George went to the animal show. They saw a great many wild beasts in cages and some with only a chain around one foot and made fast to a post.

They saw the showman go into the cage with the lion and strike him with a cowhide. The lion roared very loudly and looked cross, but he did not hurt the man.

James said, "I wish the man would come out. I do not like to see him in the cage. That big lion might eat him up, and then I would be sorry."

After they had seen the show, their kind papa took them to the bookstore and bought each of them a fine new book.

They were good boys and loved to read.

– – –

seen	chain	lion	hurt
animal	papa	eat	loved
bought	many	cross	before
show	roared	fine	beasts
kind	looked	book	James

LESSON XV (15)

The Cat and the Bird

Do not let the cat go near the bird; she will tear him with her claws and eat him up.

The cat may go and catch the mice because they do us harm and eat our food, but she must not get our poor bird because the bird sings to us and lets us know when it is time to rise.

The bird sings as soon as it is day, at the first peep of light. This bird has no seed in his box. Give him some hemp seed; it is in the bag on the high shelf. Do not spill it on the floor.

May I put this bit of sweet cake in the wires of his cage? He is like I am; he is fond of sweet cake. See how he pecks at it!

Now he goes to drink at the glass and to wash the dirt off his beak. See, you may learn even from a poor little bird that it is right to be neat and clean.

– – –

dirt	seed	shelf	wash
spill	bird	harm	clean

LESSON XVI (16)

The Duck

Have you seen the duck on her nest? She sits near the wall of the yard. She has eggs in her nest, and she sits on them to keep them warm.

And what is the use of this, do you think? Why, to make them come to life. She has been there, as you see her now, for the last ten days.

When she has kept her eggs warm in this way for four weeks, the shell of the egg will break, and the old duck will help to peck it off.

At last, out will come young live ducks, one out of each shell. Then she will have ten young ducks, for she has ten eggs in her nest.

God makes her know this and has made her love her

young so well that she does not mind the long time she must stay on her nest until they come out of the eggshell.

Have you ever seen young ducks that have just come out of the shell?

As soon as they are hatched, their mother will lead them to the water. There they can swim, and they seem to like it very much.

The ducks must love their mother and do all that she would have them do. And I dare say they will do so, for God has made them know that they must.

– – –

sits	life	stay	shell
seen	last	peck	their
duck	four	does	there
wall	born	eggs	think
yard	lead	know	break
mother	water	very	young

LESSON XVII (17)

The Good Girl

"Mamma, may I sew today?"

"Yes, my child. What do you wish to sew?"

"I wish to hem a frill for your cap. Is not this a new cap? I see it has no frill."

"You may make the frill for me. I shall like to wear a frill that you have made. Here is a bit of cloth which will make a nice frill. You must hem it. I will turn it down for you, but take care not to soil it.

"Wash your hands and take care to wipe them dry.

"Now sit down on your low stool. Now you may go on. You will see best here by my side.

"You must join these two bits with a seam. When you have done as far as this pin, bring it to me to look at."

Jane sat down upon her stool

and sewed like a little lady. In a short time she said, "Mamma, I have done as far as you told me. Will you look at it?"

"Yes, my child, it is well done, and if you take pains, as you have done today, you will soon sew well."

"I wish to sew well, Mamma, for then I can help you to make caps and frocks, and I hope to be of some use to you."

– – –

stool	cloth	wipe	these
sew	hands	dry	look
hem	frill	pains	you
new	clean	stood	hope
bits	were	seam	told
frocks	bring	soil	lady
caps	child	side	low
sat	down	has	today
like	little	short	time

LESSON XVIII (18)

About James Smith

Ann Smith had only one child, and his name was James. Ann was poor, but she did her best to work hard so that she might pay for her house and buy food and clothes.

Her house was small and stood near the road. There were two small rooms in it—one for her to sleep in and one for her to live in. She made a bed in the room she had to live in, and in this bed she put James to sleep.

In this room she had one

chair, one low stool for James to sit on, a few cups and plates, and some other things that she had bought. In the room where she slept she had her own bed and a box made of wood in which she kept her clothes.

James was so fond of her that he would run out to meet her when she came home at night from her work. When she left him to go out to work, he would sit on a large stone near the door of the hut and look at her as long as he could see her, and then he would cry and wish for her to come back to him.

James went to school, and he studied so well that in a few months he could read. Poor Ann Smith was glad her son could read, for at night when she came home from work, James would read to her in a large book which a kind friend had given him.

Someday I will tell you what was in that book, and I think you will love to hear of it and to read in it, as James Smith did.

Smith Ann James might
child poor work house
food clothes made only
room buy stool plates
things slept own fond
would meet home wood
friend large door look
come back then him
school glad months night
pay love small gone
small went had stood

LESSON XIX (19)

Albert and His Dog

Do you know Albert Ross? He has a large dog, and he calls him Dash. Dash is very black and has a long bushy tail, which he curls up over his back.

Dash is fond of Albert and

goes with him in the street, and keeps off all other dogs, and drives away the hogs, and takes good care that Albert is not hurt.

But you will laugh when I tell you that Albert calls Dash his "horse," for he does not *look* at all like a horse, but Albert has taught him to *act* like one. He has a little cart with four wheels and a little set of harness just the size to fit Dash.

Many times I have seen Albert hitch Dash to the little cart and then get in. Dash would trot off with him and go just where Albert wished.

Albert would say, "Gee, Dash!" and Dash would go to the right. Then Albert would say, "Haw, Dash!" and the dog would turn to the left. When he wanted Dash to stop, he had only to say, "Ho!" and then Albert could get out of the wagon. Is not Dash a fine dog?

– – –

size	large	only	act
turn	stop	bushy	cart
care	takes	where	Albert
calls	horse	drives	right
hitch	streets	wished	black
wheels	back	goes	Dash
laugh	taught	wanted	curls

LESSON XX (20)

The Lame Dog

One day a man took a walk in the town, and on his way home he saw a little dog which had hurt his leg.

The dog's leg hurt him so much that he could not walk on it.

When this kind man saw there was no one to take pity on the poor dog, he took him in his arms and brought him home and bound up his leg. Then he fed him and made a warm place and kept him in his house for two days.

He then sent the dog out of his house to his old home, for, as it was not his own dog, he had no right to keep him. But each day the dog came back for this kind man to dress his leg. This he did until he was quite well.

In a few weeks the dog came back once more, and with him came a dog that was lame.

The dog that had been lame and was now well, first gave the man a look, and then he gave the lame dog a look, as much as to say:

"You made my lame leg well, please do the same for this poor dog that has come with me."

— — —

day	man	went	take
town	first	home	saw
right	little	dog	gone
quite	poor	for	lame
dress	could	his	weeks
first	please	leg	look
been	kind	there	could
has	bound	same	then
good	house	and	kept

LESSON XXI (21)

The Robin

See that pretty robin! You may take your plate and put all the crumbs of bread that are left on the table on it and put it on the outside of the window. You will see how he will pick them up, for he is very hungry.

Now while he eats, I will tell you what your father and I once saw of bold or tame robins.

Some years ago one of the men who works on the farm came to tell your father that a robin had built her nest—where do you think? It was on the wagon! Was that not an odd place for her to choose?

Father and I went out to see it, and there, on the outside of that part of the wagon which is called the "bed," just over the hind wheel, was a little robin's nest, and it had four eggs in it.

The man told us that the poor bird sat on her eggs in this odd place and had not left it even though the wagon had been sent to a distant place for wood.

The wagon had just come back loaded with wood when we saw it, but the bird was not there then. She had gone off—perhaps in search of food.

Poor thing! Her nest was not left for her to hatch her eggs. Soon after we saw it, it was, by some chance, brushed off, and then the bird flew away.

	–	–	–
odd	built	think	after
just	plate	hatch	search
pick	years	crumbs	choose
bold	while	where	though
these	wheel	chance	brushed
robin	wagon	distant	perhaps

LESSON XXII (22)

Evening Prayer

At the close of the day before you go to sleep, you should not fail to pray to God to keep you from sin and from harm.

You ask your friends for food and drink and books and

clothes, and when they give you these things, you thank them and love them for the good they do you.

So you should ask your God for those things which He can give you and which no one else can give you.

You should ask Him for life and health and strength, and you should pray to Him to keep your feet from the ways of sin and shame.

You should thank Him for all His good gifts and learn, while young, to put your trust in Him. And the kind care of God will be with you, both in your youth and in your old age.

LESSON XXIII (23)

The School Girl

Jane Rice is a good girl. She goes to school every day, and she can read quite well. She does what she is told and is kind to all.

One day as she went to school, she saw a poor bee in the water on the road. So she took a leaf, for fear the bee would sting her, and held it to the bee.

The bee took hold of it with its feet, and Jane lifted it out and put it where the sun would shine on it. The bee soon got warm and flew away, and Jane was glad that she had saved its life.

LESSON XXIV (24)

The Kind Boy

James Bland found a poor, young bird on the ground. It was all wet, for there had been rain that day. "Ha!" said he, "I will have a fine pet now." So

James took it home. He met his sister Ann at the door.

"Here Ann," said he, "is a young bluebird. I found it in the road. We will put it in a cage and keep it." Ann looked at it.

"Poor thing," said she, "it is cold. Let us take it to the fire."

So she took it and warmed it. As soon as it was dry and warm, it began to chirp and try to get away.

Ann told James that it would be cruel to keep the bird. "See," Ann said, "it wants to go back to its nest. We would not like to be taken from home and kept in a cage."

James thought so, too; so he took the bird to the door. "There! go poor bird," said he. And away it flew.

Some boys would have kept it, and maybe it would have died. But James was a good boy and would not be cruel, even to a bird.

I hope that no boy or girl who reads this book will ever rob a bird's nest.

– – –

cold	have	back	warm
taken	sister	ground	nest
way	maybe	dry	rain
cage	the	thing	poor
cruel	reads	bird	flew
looked	kept	though	door
began	good	boy	who
bluebird	ever	very	found

LESSON XXV (25)

Mary's Lamb

Mary had a little lamb,
Its fleece was white as snow,
And everywhere that Mary went
The lamb was sure to go.

He went with her to school one
day;
That was against the rule;
It made the children laugh and
play,
To see a lamb at school.

So the teacher turned him out,
But still he lingered near,
And waited patiently about,
Till Mary did appear.

And then he ran to her and laid
His head upon her arm,
As if he said, I'm not afraid,
You'll keep me from all harm.

"What makes the lamb love
Mary so?"
The eager children cry;
"O Mary loves the lamb, you
know,"
The teacher did reply.

And you, each gentle animal
To you, for life, may bind,
And make it follow at your call,
If you are always kind.

– – –

laid	lamb	where	follow
rule	what	fleece	every
that	harm	school	waited
love	made	eager	appear
sure	snow	Mary	against
bind	white	gentle	animal

LESSON XXVI (26)

The Happy Return

Mary and Martha were two sisters who dwelt in a village near the sea. Their parents were both dead, and their brother John was far away at sea.

They worked hard with their

needles and prayed God to protect them and to bless their labor. They never missed going to church nor ever failed to pray for their brother's safe return.

One fine summer morning they went, as they often did, to the beach to view the sun rise upon the water. This is always a grand sight, but this morning they thought the sun seemed to shine with more splendor than it had done for the past week.

The sea was calm and still, but though they strained their eyes to see if any ship might be passing by, not a sail was to be seen, and both sighed as they thought of their brother John, and turned to go home.

They had walked a little way in silence when Martha said, "Dear Mary, I was just thinking how kind God has always been to us and was wishing that it might please Him to send John home to us this very day. What a day of joy it would be then!"

And such a joyous day it was to them both, for no sooner had they left the beach, than the good ship Rover came into sight. Her crew had all been paid, and John stepped on shore with a light heart. His discharge was in its tin case and his pocket was full of gold. It was, indeed, a happy day for the two loving sisters.

\- \- \-

village	each	their	splendor
sail	joyous	gold	shore
grand	sigh	strain	view
crew	hearts	protect	summer
calm	sight	church	needles

LESSON XXVII (27)

The New Slate

Little Charles had a new slate given him. It was bought for him by his father so that he might learn numbers. One day he made some pictures on his slate.

Look, I have drawn a boy on my new slate. See what a long nose he has! Ah! He has but one arm.

There, I have drawn a pig and a hen and a duck. Why, the pig has but two legs and the duck has four. Well, I can rub out two of the duck's legs and give them to the pig.

There, now I will draw a man with a whip in his hand. The man has come to put the pig in the pen.

Why, the man is not as tall as the pig. I must rub them all out, for they are not well done.

And here is Betty, the maid; she has come to take me to bed. Well, if it is time, I must go. I will put my slate away that I may have it safe when next I want to draw.

LESSON XXVIII (28)

How To Add

John: I wish I could add, as James does. May I get a slate and try?

Mother: You cannot use a slate yet; but I will teach you how to add with these beans. Now listen to what I say to you. Here is one, and here are two more. How many do one bean and two beans make?

Put them in your left hand and count them this way—one, two, three. You see that one and two make three.

Now take three more beans and add them to those in your left hand and count them all—one, two, three, four, five, six. Three and three make six.

Now take four beans and add two more to them. You see there are six. Four and two are six. Now take five beans and add one to them. You see there are six. So five and one make six.

LESSON XXIX (29)

The Storyteller

Peter Pindar was a great storyteller. This is known to all children who have read his books. One day as he was going by the school, the children came around him, and they all wished him to tell them a new story.

"Well," said Peter, "I love to please good children, and as you all appear kind and civil, I will tell you a story which you have never heard. But before we begin, let us go and sit down in a cool, shady place.

"And now, master John, you must be as still as a little mouse. And Mary, you must be careful not to let Towser bark and make a noise.

"A long way from this place in a land where it is very cold, and where much snow falls, and where the hills are so high that their tops appear to reach the sky, there live some men whose joy it is to help folks who pass by these hills.

"These men keep large dogs, which they teach to go out and hunt for persons who may be lost in the snowdrifts. The dogs have so fine a scent or smell that they can find folks by means of it, even when it is too dark to see, or when the folks they go out to hunt for lie hidden in the deep snowdrifts."

– – –

whose	teller	story	Pindar
much	have	books	Towser
great	read	going	Mary
please	begin	down	master
appear	high	these	wished
persons	drifts	scent	never
children	hid	deep	careful
shady	around	hills	snow

LESSON XXX (30)

The Snow Dog and Boy

The storyteller continued with his story.

"One sad cold night when the snow fell fast and the wind blew loud and shrill, and it was quite dark, with not a star to be seen in the sky, these good men sent out a dog to hunt for those who might need help.

"In an hour or two the dog was heard at the gate. When they went to look out, they saw the dog there with a boy on his back.

"The poor child was stiff with cold and could hardly hold on to the dog's back.

"He told the men that he had lain a long time in the snow and was too ill and weak to walk, and the snow had fallen fast on him. At length, he felt some-thing pull him by the coat, and then he heard the bark of a dog close by him.

"The boy then put out his hand, and he felt the hair of the dog; then the dog gave him one more pull. This gave the poor boy some hope, and he took hold of the dog and drew himself out of the snow, but he felt that he could not stand or walk.

"He then got upon the dog's back and put his arms around the dog's neck, and thus he held on. He felt sure the dog did not mean to hurt him. Thus he rode on the dog's back all the way to the house of the good men, who took care of the boy until the snow was gone. Then they sent him to his own home."

– – –

back	after	heard	home
might	neck	length	could
snow	something	mean	quite

LESSON XXXI (31)

Good Advice

If you have done anything during the day that is wrong, ask forgiveness of God and your parents.

Remember that you should learn some good thing every day. If you have learned nothing all day, that day is lost.

If anyone has done you wrong, before you go to sleep, forgive him in your heart. Do not go to sleep with hatred in your heart toward anyone.

Never speak to anyone in an angry or harsh voice.

If you have spoken unkind words to a brother or sister, go and ask forgiveness.

If you have disobeyed your parents, go and confess it.

Ask God to aid you always to do good and avoid evil.

– – –

before	parents	during	always
brother	forgive	unkind	forgiveness
hatred	confess	sister	remember

LESSON XXXII (32)

Little Lucy

Lucy, can you read?

Yes, sir, I can.

Would you rather read than play?

Yes, sir, I would because Mamma tells me that play will not be of any use to me after I grow up, but if I love to read I will be wise and good.

A little boy or girl who cannot read is not much better than Puss. Puss can run and play as well as they, but Puss can never learn to read. Boys and girls who do not know how to read cannot learn anything except what is told to them.

But when boys or girls know how to read, they can sit down and learn a great deal when there is no one to talk to them.

After boys and girls have learned to read, they can learn to write. Then they can send letters to their friends who live far away.

LESSON XXXIII (33)

Peter Holt

Peter Holt was left at home one day by his parents when they went out to take a ride.

His mother told him to stay in the house until she came

back. "Be very sure that you do not go out among the horses," said she. "They may hurt you."

Peter said he would do as he was told. So his mother kissed him and left. He soon got very tired of staying in the house, so he went to the door and soon after, ran down into the lot to look at a little colt which his father had given him.

It was very tame, so he put his hand on its neck, and then on its head. At last he thought it was so tame and gentle that he would ride it. He led it to the fence and jumped on its back.

The colt had never before felt anything on its back and was very much alarmed. It put down its head and ran off at a great rate and at last kicked up its hind feet and threw Peter over its head.

Peter was badly hurt, but he crept home as well as he could. If he had been so badly hurt as not to be able to get home, he might have died in the field before his parents came home.

Little children may learn from this that they should always obey their parents. How many little girls and boys have been hurt because they did not do as they were told!

– – –

their	children	down	obey
kissed	should	back	given
went	crept	parents	hurt
field	much	house	over
started	that	always	because
tame	when	kicked	alarmed
learn	gentle	badly	rate

LESSON XXXIV (34)

Mr. Post and the Little Girl

One cold night after old Mr. Post had gone to bed, he heard a noise at the door. So he got up and went out.

And what do you think he found? A dog? No. A goat? No.

He found a little baby girl on the steps.

Some bad person had left her there, and if Mr. Post had not taken her into the house, she might have died with cold. He held her by the fire until she was warm and then he took her in his arms and went to bed.

How kind old Mr. Post was. He did not know what to do with the innocent little baby, but he could not let her die.

When Mr. Post's little friends came to see him the next day, they thought it very strange to see him have a little baby with him. He told them how he got the baby, and they all said that they would bring her milk and sometimes come and help to take care of her.

The little girl was named Mary. She was soon very fond of Mr. Post and called him "Papa." In a short time she grew so large that she could run and open the gate for her papa when he was going out.

Mr. Post taught her to read, and at night Mary would read the Bible to her papa.

Mary was soon able to get the dinner and do little chores;

and when her papa got so old that he could not work, Mary took care of him.

– – –

Mary	until	called	sometimes
going	dinner	papa	innocent
died	open	into	person
baby	friends	could	chores

LESSON XXXV (35)

Mary and Her Kid

A little girl who lived in a place where there are a great many goats took a walk one day and found a little kid.

The old goat, the mother of the little kid, had left it, and it was almost dead.

Mary felt sorry for the poor little thing; so she took it up in her arms, and carried it home with her. Her mother let her keep the kid for her own. Mary got some clean straw and laid it on the warm hearth for a bed for the kid. She warmed some milk and held it to him to drink.

The kid drank it and then lay down and took a fine nap. The next day Mary named her kid Tom. Tom soon learned to follow Mary about the house and trot by her side into the yard. He would run races with her in the field, feed out of her hand, and was a great pet at all times.

One fine warm day, after Mary had done her morning work, she went out to play with her kid. She looked about the house door and could not see

Tom. She then ran to the field and called, "Tom! Tom!"

But Tom had found a flock of goats and was playing with them. He loved to stay with them better than with Mary. Mary went home crying, and it was a long time before she forgot her little Tom.

LESSON XXXVI (36)

The Little Dog

I like to see a little dog,
And pat him on the head;
So prettily he wags his tail,
Whenever he is fed.

Some little dogs are very good,
And very useful too;
And do you know that they will mind
What they are bid to do?

Then I will never beat my dog,
And never give him pain;

Poor fellow! I will give him food,
And he will love me then.

LESSON XXXVII (37)

The Fireside

One winter's night James was reading to his mother and sisters as they sat by a fine fire. The little girls were sewing, and their mother was busy at her spinning wheel.

At last James finished the chapter and Emma, looking up, said, "Mother, I think your wheel hums very sweetly tonight."

"And it seems to me," said Mary, "as if the fire were

brighter than usual. How I love to hear it crackle!"

"And I was just going to say," cried James, "that this is a better candle than we had last night."

"My dears," said their mother, "I have no doubt that you feel more than usually happy tonight, and perhaps that is the reason why you think the hum of the wheel sweeter, the fire better, and the candlelight brighter than they were last night."

"But, Mother," said Mary, "I don't see why we are happier

now, than we were last night. For last night cousin Jane was here, and we played 'Puss-in-the-Corner' and 'Blind Man' until we were all tired."

"I know! I know!" shouted James. "It is because we have been doing something *useful* tonight. Mary, you and Emma have been making a dress for the poor woman who lives at the end of the lane, and I have been reading a good book. We all feel happy because we have been busy."

"You are right, my son," their mother said, "and I am glad you have all learned that there is something more pleasant than play, and, at the same time, much more instructing."

– – –

fire	fine	lives	useful
lane	last	right	sisters
hear	they	night	candle
than	poor	dress	played
were	book	there	sewing
more	blind	busy	chapter
hums	doubt	cousin	brighter
know	wheel	sweeter	pleasant

LESSON XXXVIII (38)

The Thick Shade

Come, let us go into the thick shade, for it is noonday and the summer sun beats hot upon our heads.

The shade is pleasant and cool; the branches meet above our heads and shut out the sun as with a green curtain.

The grass is soft to our feet, and the clear brook washes the roots of the trees.

The cattle can lie down to sleep in the cool shade, but we can do better; we can raise our voices to heaven; we can praise the great God who made us.

He made the warm sun and the cool shade, the trees that grow upwards, and the brooks that run along.

The plants and trees are made to give fruit to man.

All that live get life from God.

– – –

come	noon	thick	shade
heads	clear	cattle	voices
raise	pleasant	heaven	summer

LESSON XXXIX (39)

About the Moon

The moon is very large.

See how beautiful it looks.

The moon is round now because it is a full moon.

But it will not be so round tomorrow night. It will lose a little, and the next night a little more, and so on, until it is like a bow when it is bent. It will not be seen until after you are in bed. It will grow less and less until in two weeks there will be no moon at all.

Then after that, there will be a new moon. You will see it just before night, and it will be very thin at first.

But it will grow more round and larger each night until at last, in two weeks more, it will be a full moon again like this. And you will see it rise again behind the trees in four weeks from this time, just as you see it now.

If we had no moon, it would be very dark at night. We could not see to walk or do anything.

When there is snow on the ground and the moon shines, it

is almost as bright as day. But when there is no moon and the stars do not shine, it is very dark.

– – –

moon	lose	weeks	again
until	little	new	because

LESSON XL (40)

The Boy Who Told a Lie—Part I

There was once a boy whose father sent him to ride a few miles upon an errand and told him not to stop by the way. It was a fine sunny morning, and as he rode by the green trees and heard the sweet songs of the birds, he seemed to feel as happy as they.

After he had done his errand, he started to come home. As he was riding by a house where two of his playmates lived, he thought he would stop a few moments to see them. The boy stayed longer and longer until two hours had been spent in play.

With a heavy heart he now mounted his horse again. He rode slowly along thinking what excuse he should make to his father for not coming home sooner.

The boy trembled and turned pale as he saw his father. When his kind father came up to him, he said, "Father, I lost the road, and it took me some time to get back again, and that is the reason why I have been gone so long."

His father had never known him to be guilty of a lie before and believed what his son told him. But oh, how guilty and ashamed did that boy feel as he walked along by his father. His look of innocence was gone, and he was ashamed to look his father or his mother in the face. He tried to appear easy and happy, but he was uneasy and miserable.

– – –

miles	errand	sunny	morning
green	playmates	lived	moments
stay	hours	spent	heavy
mount	excuse	sooner	trembled
pale	lost	reason	known
guilty	ashamed	appear	miserable

LESSON XLI (41)

The Boy Who Told a Lie—Part II

When the little boy, whom you last read about, went to bed that night, he was afraid. He knew that he had done wrong, and it was long before he could quiet his troubled spirit with sleep.

Thus things went on for two or three weeks. One day a man called to see the father of this boy on business, and as soon as the boy saw him come into the house, his heart beat quick, and he turned pale. He feared that something would be said that would bring the whole story to light.

After talking a few moments with his father, the man turned to the little boy, and said, "Well, how did you get home the other day? My boys had a very pleasant visit from you."

Can you think how this boy felt? You could have almost heard his heart beat. The blood rushed into his face, and he could not speak, and he dared not raise his eyes from the floor.

The man then turned to his

father and said, "You must let your son come up again and see my boys. When he was there about two weeks ago, he only stayed about two hours, and they hoped he had come to spend the whole day with them."

Now the whole truth was out. The boy stood before his parents covered with shame. How bitterly had he suffered. The guilty boy burst into tears and implored his parents' forgiveness.

But he was told by his parents that he had sinned, not

only against them, but also against God. The humble child went to God in penitence and in prayer. He made a full confession of all to his parents and obtained their forgiveness. It was not until then that peace of mind was restored.

– – –

when	shame	almost	penitence
whole	them	guilty	confession
weeks	peace	humble	covered
soon	truth	pleasant	obtained
said	must	turned	business
could	come	sinned	implored
floor	spend	parents	forgiveness

LESSON XLII (42)

John Jones

John Jones was a good boy, but he could not read nor write. His mother was poor and could not pay for him to go to school; so she sent him out to help a man at the side of the road to break stones. John could not earn much, it is true, yet it was good for him to be at work.

It is good for us all to have work to do. It is bad for us not to work. John was a good boy, and he did not love to play so much that he could not work.

No, he knew it to be right to work, and when his work was done, he would play.

The man for whom John worked was very kind to John and gave him a great deal of good advice.

One day he said to him: John, you must always bear in mind that it was God who made you and who gave you all that you have and all that you hope for. He gave you life and food and a home to live in.

All who take care of you and help you were sent you by God. He sent his Son to show you

His will and to die for your sake.

He gave you His word to let you know what He has done for you and what He wants you to do.

He sees you in the dark as well as in the daylight. He can tell all that you do, and all that you say, and all that is in your mind.

Oh! ever seek this God. Pray to Him when you rise and when you lie down. Keep His day, hear His word, and do His will, for He loves you and will be your God forever.

– – –

have	you	hope	has
pray	die	word	help
done	life	sent	read
food	bear	that	mind
your	live	whom	ever
work	good	show	dark
very	advice	day	loves
kind	always	know	seek
great	some	him	deal
gave	sees	down	hope

LESSON XLIII (43)

Story About Ralph Wick

Ralph Wick was five years old and in most things he was a fine boy. But he was too apt to cry when he could not have his own way.

This was wrong. All good boys and girls know that they should take what their kind friends see fit to give them and be glad to get it.

But Ralph did not think of this. All he thought of, was how to get what he wanted to have. If he was told that it was not right for him to have it or that it would do him harm, he would say, "I *will* have it." And then, if he did not get it, he was sure to cry.

One day he went with his nurse into the fields. The sun shone brightly, the grass was cut, the plants in bloom were of all colors; and Ralph thought he was, for once, a good boy. A smile was on his face, and he felt a wish to do as he was told.

So he said, "Nurse, I will be good now and do as you bid me; now please help me to toss this hay."

"That I will," said the nurse. And they threw the hay as Ralph wished, until he said he was tired and must sit down to rest.

"You have been so good a boy," said the nurse, "that if you will sit here, I will go to the hedge and get a nice red rose for you."

"I should like very much to have one," said Ralph, "and if you will get it for me, I will not move till you come back."

The nurse soon brought the rose and gave it to him. "Thank you, my kind nurse," said he. "I like this sweet, red rose. But I see you have a *white* one, too. Please give that to me."

The nurse said, "No, my dear. I only brought this white rose to show you how many thorns it has on its stem. You must take care not to touch one of this kind. If you should try to pluck a white rose like this, you would be sure to hurt your hand."

Now what do you think Ralph did? I will tell you. He found it very easy to be good when he had everything he wanted. But as soon as the nurse told him he must not have the white rose, he began to scream, and snatched it.

But he was soon very sorry for what he had done. The thorns on the stem of the rose tore the skin of his hand, and it was sore for a long time.

After this, when he wanted what it was not best for him to have, his nurse would point to his sore hand, and Ralph at last learned to do as he was told and became a much better and happier boy.

cry	five	pluck	easy
apt	girls	touch	tired
toss	right	think	sorry
tore	years	move	colors
sore	nurse	fields	every
was	threw	thorn	wanted
most	hedge	please	learned
wish	Ralph	scream	brightly
know	wrong	brought	snatched

LESSON XLIV (44)

Butterflies

Butterflies are pretty things!
  Prettier than you or I,
See the colors on their wings!
  Who would hurt a butterfly?

Softly! softly! girls and boys;
He'll come near us by and by;
Here he is! Don't make a noise!
We'll not hurt you, butterfly.

Not to hurt a living thing,
Let all young children try;
See, again he's on the wing;
Goodby! Pretty butterfly!

LESSON XLV (45)

Good Sense and Pride

Ann had a new dress, of which she thought much more than a good girl ought to have done. She was so proud of it that she could not think of her books, and off she went to Grace, to show her new clothes.

She found Grace where her pinks grew at the back of the house in which she lived. Grace ran to meet Ann with a smile and said, "I am quite glad you have come, for my rosebush is in bloom, and you shall have the best flower on it."

"Thank you," said Ann, as she looked at her dress, "but this sleeve hurts my arm. Do you think it quite fits me?"

"I should think not if it hurts you," said Grace, "and, if you please, you can take it off, and I will lend you one of mine while you stay."

Grace meant this as she said it. She did not think that Ann had spoken of the tight sleeve only that she should praise the dress.

"What ails you, Ann?" said Grace, "you look as though you could cry. If the dress hurts you, you shall not keep it on; come, let us change it."

"Oh! Grace," said Ann, as the tears fell fast from her eyes, "it is not the dress that hurts me, but my *pride*. But I will tell you all my faults and will try to be as good and as kind as you are, for the time to come."

Ann kept her word, and though she found it a hard thing at first, to give up her love of dress, yet *good sense* at last taught her that the sure way to be happy was to be good.

– – –

ails	tears	smile	tight
rose	pinks	dress	faults
mine	pride	dwelt	books
sense	ought	bloom	meant
Grace	proud	praise	please
sleeve	taught	change	flower

LESSON XLVI (46)

The Little Chimney Sweep

Part I

Some time ago there was a little chimney sweep who had to sweep a chimney in the house of a very rich lady. The little sweep went up at the kitchen fireplace and came down in the bedroom.

When he got into the bedroom, he found himself all alone. He stopped a moment to look around upon the rich furniture. As he looked on the top of the table, he saw an elegant, gold watch with gold seals to it.

He had never seen anything so beautiful before, and he took it up in his hands. As he listened to hear it tick, it began to play sweet music. He then thought, if it only belonged to him, how rich he would be. And then he thought he might hide it in his blanket.

Now, said he, if I take it, I shall be a thief—and yet, nobody sees me. Nobody! Does not God see me? Could I ever again be good? Could I then ever say my prayers again to God? And what should I do when I come to die?

– – –

chimney	sweep	house	rich
kitchen	fireplace	alone	bedroom
furniture	table	elegant	watch
thought	blanket	hide	prayers
sweet	again	music	tick
moment	play	stopped	thief

LESSON XLVII (47)

The Little Chimney Sweep

Part II

While the little chimney sweep was thinking about taking the lady's gold watch, he felt cold all over and trembled with fear.

"No," said he, "I cannot take this watch. I would rather be a sweep and always be poor, than steal." And down he laid the watch and crept up the chimney.

Now the lady who owned the watch was just in the next room, and she could look through and see and hear all that passed. She did not say anything to the boy then, but let him go away.

The next day she sent for him, and when he came, she said to him, "Well, my little friend, why did you not take my watch yesterday?" The little sweep then fell upon his knees and told the lady all about it.

Now, as the little sweep did not steal the gold watch nor tell any stories about it, the lady let him stay and live in her house. For many years she gave him good instruction, and when he grew up he was a good, pious man and always tried to remember the commandment which says, "Thou shalt not steal."

Here we see the truth of the old saying, "Honesty is the best policy." Had this sweep taken the lady's watch, he would have stolen. Then he would have been sent to jail. He would also have sinned against God, and perhaps, never have become pious.

Let no little boy or girl ever take things that are not theirs, for it is stealing, and they who steal are thieves.

Some children seem to think that to take an apple or an orange or some other small thing without permission is no sin. But they are mistaken.

You cannot steal the smallest pin without its being a sin nor without being seen by that eye which never sleeps.

– – –

pious	become	remember
policy	perhaps	yesterday
knees	stealing	permission
orange	smallest	instructed
stories	mistaken	commandment

LESSON XLVIII (48)

Don't Take Strong Drink

No little boys or girls should ever drink rum or whiskey unless they want to become drunkards.

Men who drink strong drink are glad to have any excuse for doing it. So, one will drink it because he is so hot. Another will drink it because he is so cold.

One will drink it when he is wet and another, because he is dry. One will drink it because he is alone. And another will put it into his glass of water to kill the insects.

Thus the pure water from the brook is poisoned with the "drunkard's drink," and the man who uses it becomes a sot. Then he is seen tottering through the streets, a shame to himself and to all his family.

And oh, how dreadful to die a drunkard. The Bible says that no drunkard shall inherit the kingdom of heaven.

Whiskey makes the happy miserable, and it causes the rich to become poor.

LESSON XLIX (49)

The Little Star

Twinkle, twinkle, little star,
How I wonder what you are;
Up above the world so high,
Like a diamond in the sky.

When the blazing sun is set,
And the grass with dew is wet,
Then you show your little light:
Twinkle, twinkle, all the night!

Then if I were in the dark.
I would thank you for your
spark:

I could not see which way to go,
If you did not twinkle so.

And when I am sound asleep,
Oft you through my window peep,
For you never shut your eye,
Till the sun is in the sky.

– – –

eye	world	star	asleep
sky	wonder	window	spark

LESSON L (50)

Speak the Truth

One day Anna thought she would take a walk instead of going to school. But she saw that her mother was watching her from the window.

So she went along the road and turned round the corner that led to the schoolhouse, so that her mother might think she was going there. Was not this lying?

Anna took a long walk and came home about the time when the scholars came back from school. Her mother thought she had been at school, and her teacher thought she must be sick. So, you see, she deceived them both.

One day while Anna was out, her uncle and aunt and little cousin came to see her mother. They lived a great way off and did not come very often. They said they were going away over the wide ocean to England and did not expect ever to come back.

As they were to leave in an hour or two, they wished to see Anna. Her mother sent to school for her to come home. Her teacher sent back word that she was not there and had not been for two or three days! So her uncle and aunt and cousin had to go away without bidding her goodby.

When Anna came home, her mother said, "Where have you been, Anna?" The little girl hung down her head and did not say anything; for she saw from her mother's look that she knew all about her deceit.

The deceitful little girl was then told that her uncle and aunt and cousin had gone away without seeing her and that they were never coming back.

Anna cried very much for she loved them dearly and said she would never again either act or speak another lie.

– – –

sick	aunt	gone	speak
saw	been	walk	school
road	wide	home	thought
hour	hung	while	uncle
house	knew	might	lying
either	dearly	coming	deceit

LESSON LI (51)

The Sheep

Lazy sheep, pray tell me why,
In the pleasant fields you lie,
Eating grass and daisies white,
From the morning till the night?
Everything can something do,
But of what kind of use are you?

Nay, my little master, nay,
Do not serve me so, I pray;
Don't you see the wool that grows
On my back, to make you clothes?
Cold, oh, very cold you'd be,
If I did not give it thee.

Sure it seems a pleasant thing,
Nipping daisies in the spring;
But how many days I pass
On the cold and dewy grass;
Or I get my dinner where
All the ground is brown and bare.

Then the farmer comes at last,
When the merry spring is past,
Cuts my woolly coat away,
For your clothes in wintry day.
Little master, this is why
In the pleasant fields I lie.

cuts	seems	serve	lazy
coat	brown	fields	dewy
wool	comes	grows	eating
sheep	spring	clothes	daisies
farmer	nipping	pleasant	master

LESSON LII (52)

The Broken Window—Part I

George Ellet had a fine New Year's gift. What do you think it was? A bright silver dollar! A merry boy was George when he thought of all the fine things he might buy with it. And as soon as the sun began to make the air feel a little warm, he put on his cap and gloves and ran into the street.

The ground was covered with snow, but the sun shone out and everything looked bright. As George went skipping along, he met some boys who were throwing snowballs. This is fine sport, and George pulled off his gloves and was soon as busy as the rest.

He gathered up the snow and pressed it between his hands to make it into balls. Soon he was throwing snowballs with the boys. Suddenly he hit James Mason. But the ball was soft and James was not hurt. He made another snowball and again aimed it at James. Away went the ball! But it missed James and broke a window on the other side of the street. George was afraid that some-one would come out of the house and whip him; so he ran off as fast as he could.

As soon as he got around the next corner, he stopped because he was very sorry for what he had done. Just then he saw a man carrying a box with glass doors; it was full of pretty toys. Because George was only eight years old, he forgot the broken window and ran after the man.

– – –

toys	eight	after	between
buy	soon	other	silver
soft	sport	bright	merry
whip	broke	gloves	forgot
street	skipping	throwing	covered

LESSON LIII (53)

The Broken Window—Part II

As George was about to buy a little toy house with doors and chimneys, and as he put his hand into his pocket for the money, he thought of the broken window. Then he said to himself, "I have no right to spend this dollar for a toy house. I ought to go back and pay for the glass I broke with my snowball."

So he gave back the house to the toy man and turned around. But he was afraid of being scolded or beaten and did not know what to do. He went up and down the street and felt very badly. He wished to buy something nice with his money; and he also wished to pay for the glass he had broken.

At last he said to himself, "It was wrong to break the window although I did not mean to do it. I will go and pay the man for it at once. If it takes all my money, I will try not to be sorry; and I do not think the man will hurt me if I offer to pay for the mischief I have done." He then started off and felt much happier for having made up his mind to do what was right.

He rang the doorbell, and when the man came out, George said, "Sir, I threw a snowball through your window. But I did not intend to do it and am very sorry, and I wish to pay you. Here is the dollar my father gave me as a New Year's gift this morning."

The man took the dollar and asked George if he had any more money. George said he had not. "Well," said the man, "this will be enough." So after asking George where he lived and what was his name, he called him an honest lad and shut the door.

\- - -

gift	rang	ought	dollar
door	glass	wrong	money
once	right	thought	honest
mean	threw	scolded	beaten
intend	enough	morning	mischief
offer	sorry	nice	chimneys

LESSON LIV (54)

The Broken Window—Part III

When George had paid the man, he ran away and felt very happy because he had done what he knew to be right. He played very merrily all the forenoon, although he had no money to spend, and went home at dinner time with a face as rosy and eyes as bright as if nothing had gone wrong.

At dinner Mr. Ellet asked George what he had bought with his money. George very honestly told him all about the broken window and said he felt very well without any money to spend. When dinner was over, Mr. Ellet told George to go and look in his hat.

He did so, and found *two* silver dollars. The man whose window had been broken had been there and told George's father about it. He also gave back the dollar which George had paid him, and *another one* with it.

A few months after that, the man came and told Mr. Ellet that he wanted a good boy to stay in his store and would like to have George, as soon as he left school, for he was sure that George was an *honest* boy. George went to live with this man, who was a rich merchant. In a few years he became the merchant's partner and is now rich. George often thinks of the *broken window.*

– – –

felt	store	years	dinner
rich	knew	would	played
paid	spend	bought	became
eyes	rosy	months	wanted
partner	forenoon	merchant	honest

GOODBY

Now my little readers, we have come to the end of the book, and I must bid you good-by. But before we part, let me give you a little advice.

You are now a little child; you are but a few years old and have not much wisdom. Therefore, always listen to your teacher and to your parents. They are older than you, and they know better what is for your good.

Little children, you must love your parents. You should

be kind to your teachers and gentle to your brothers and sisters and playmates. Use no hard words, be guilty of no ill-natured tricks, and tell no ill-natured tales.

Always do to other children as you wish them to do by you. This is the "Golden Rule"— Remember it when you play. Act upon it now, and when you are grown up, do not forget it.

If you have been a good child and learned your lessons well, you may now have the *Second Reader*.

WILLIAM HOLMES McGUFFEY

On the campus of Miami University in Oxford, Ohio, stands the old McGuffey house. Now a museum and National Historic Landmark, the house honors William Holmes McGuffey, the American educator who earned the title, "Schoolmaster to the Nation." In this house nearly 150 years ago, McGuffey wrote his influential and often imitated ECLECTIC READERS.

William McGuffey was born September 23, 1800, to a Scotch-Irish Presbyterian family. When he was two years old, his family moved from Pennsylvania into the newly-opened Northwest Territory, near what is now Youngstown, Ohio.

The rigors of the frontier during his formative years and his family's Calvinist heritage molded his life and his outlook. Also, at different times in his early teens and mid-twenties, he lived in the homes of Presbyterian ministers who served as tutors and mentors for the young man.

McGuffey began teaching in a rural school when he was 13. He continued his own studies, however, and graduated from Washington College in Pennsylvania. From there he went on to teach in a private school in Paris, Kentucky.

When McGuffey was 26, he became professor of ancient languages at Miami University. Three years later, he was ordained as a Presbyterian minister.

But McGuffey always remained in education.

In 1835, McGuffey contracted to write reading books for schoolchildren. The following year, he sat at an octagonal table he had designed himself, gathered his material and wrote what would be the first four McGuffey READERS.

McGuffey later served as president of Cincinnati College and of Ohio University. His final position—which he held 28 years—was professor of philosophy at the University of Virginia.

McGuffey married Harriet Holmes during his 10 years at Miami University. They had four children.

McGuffey died May 4, 1873, and was buried at Charlottesville, Virginia.

THE McGUFFEY READERS

To understand the many McGuffey editions that have appeared through the years, one must know that the READERS have undergone several revisions—two of them major. But not all the READERS bearing McGuffey's name were produced or approved by him.

William McGuffey wrote, compiled and published the first four READERS in 1836 and 1837. His brother Alexander was primarily responsible for the fifth and sixth McGuffey READERS.

The 1843 and 1853 revisions of the first four READERS were made by Dr. T. S. Pinneo but seen and approved by McGuffey, who was by then teaching at the University of Virginia.

As the character of the public schools was becoming more secular, however, textbook publishers determined their market was becoming less interested in McGuffey's strong accent on moral and spiritual values. McGuffey neither contributed to nor approved of the revisions made in 1857 and 1879. The 1879 edition, still published today under a 1920 copyright, contained only those lessons reflecting the morality and lifestyle of an emerging middle class. The emphasis on righteousness, piety and salvation was gone.

The original McGuffey READERS were not titled to indicate grade levels. In the multiple grade schools of the day, each student progressed at his own pace. Attempts to equate READER names with grade levels were not made until the 1879 revision.

McGuffey intended many uses for the word lists (such as spelling, new words, etc.), but, there is not one with every lesson.

Also, the early McGuffey READERS are far more demanding than later editions. Because students then would leave school permanently at a young age, the students' interests were challenged early. For many years, anyone who had finished the fourth READER was considered very well educated.

BIBLIOGRAPHY

Lindberg, Stanley W. *The Annotated McGuffey: Selections from the McGuffey Eclectic Readers 1836–1920.* New York: Van Nostrand Reinhold Co., 1976.

Niety, John. *Old Textbooks.* Pittsbury: University of Pittsbury Press, 1961.

Smith, William E. *William Holmes McGuffey.* A pamphlet printed by the McGuffey Museum of Miami University, Oxford, Ohio, 1973.

Vail, Henry H. *A History of the McGuffey Readers.* Cleveland: Burrows Brothers, 1911.

Westerhoff, John III. *McGuffey and His Readers: Piety, Morality, and Education in Nineteenth-Century America.* Nashville: Abingdon, 1978.